THE RIGHT TO VOTE

BLACK AMERICANS' RIGHT TO VOTE

by Anitra Budd

Ideas for Parents and Teachers

Pogo Books let children practice reading informational text while introducing them to nonfiction features such as headings, labels, sidebars, maps, and diagrams, as well as a table of contents, glossary, and index.

Carefully leveled text with a strong photo match offers early fluent readers the support they need to succeed.

Before Reading

- "Walk" through the book and point out the various nonfiction features. Ask the student what purpose each feature serves.
- Look at the glossary together. Read and discuss the words.

Read the Book

- Have the child read the book independently.
- Invite him or her to list questions that arise from reading.

After Reading

- Discuss the child's questions. Talk about how he or she might find answers to those questions.
- Prompt the child to think more. Ask: What did you know about the history of Black Americans' voting rights before reading this book? What more would you like to learn?

Pogo Books are published by Jump!
5357 Penn Avenue South
Minneapolis, MN 55419
www.jumplibrary.com

Library of Congress Cataloging-in-Publication Data

Names: Budd, Anitra, author.
Title: Black Americans' right to vote / by Anitra Budd.
Description: Minneapolis, MN: Jump!, Inc., [2025]
Series: The right to vote | Includes index.
Audience: Ages 7-10
Identifiers: LCCN 2023058848 (print)
LCCN 2023058849 (ebook)
ISBN 9798892131438 (hardcover)
ISBN 9798892131445 (paperback)
ISBN 9798892131452 (ebook)
Subjects: LCSH: African Americans–Suffrage–History–Juvenile literature. | United States. Voting Rights Act of 1965. | Elections–Corrupt practices–United States–Juvenile literature. | Voter intimidation–United States–Juvenile literature. | African Americans–Civil rights–History–Juvenile literature. | Social justice–United States–History–Juvenile literature. | United States–Race relations–History–Juvenile literature.
Classification: LCC JK1924 .B83 2025 (print)
LCC JK1924 (ebook)
DDC 324.6/2–dc23/eng/20240130
LC record available at https://lccn.loc.gov/2023058848
LC ebook record available at https://lccn.loc.gov/2023058849

Editor: Alyssa Sorenson
Designer: Molly Ballanger

Photo Credits: ViDI Studio/Shutterstock, cover (man); Mega Pixel/Shutterstock, cover (sticker); YinYang/iStock, cover (sign); fstop123/iStock, 1; ImagePixel/Shutterstock, 3; adamkaz/iStock, 4; SDI Productions/iStock, 5; Rowland Scherman/National Archives/Interim Archives/Getty, 6-7; duncan1890/iStock, 8; Bettmann/Getty, 9, 12-13; Getty Images, 10-11; World History Archive/Image Asset Management/SuperStock, 14-15; Adam Parent/Shutterstock, 16; Rob Crandall/Alamy, 17; Jim West/Alamy, 18-19; Dustin Chambers/Bloomberg/Getty, 20-21; Marion S. Trikosko/Library of Congress, 23.

Printed in the United States of America at Corporate Graphics in North Mankato, Minnesota.

TABLE OF CONTENTS

CHAPTER 1

WHAT IS VOTING?

The United States is a **democracy**. U.S. **citizens** vote in **elections**. They pick leaders. Leaders run our cities, states, and country. They make laws people want.

People vote using **ballots**. The votes are counted. The **candidate** with the most votes wins!

1963 protest

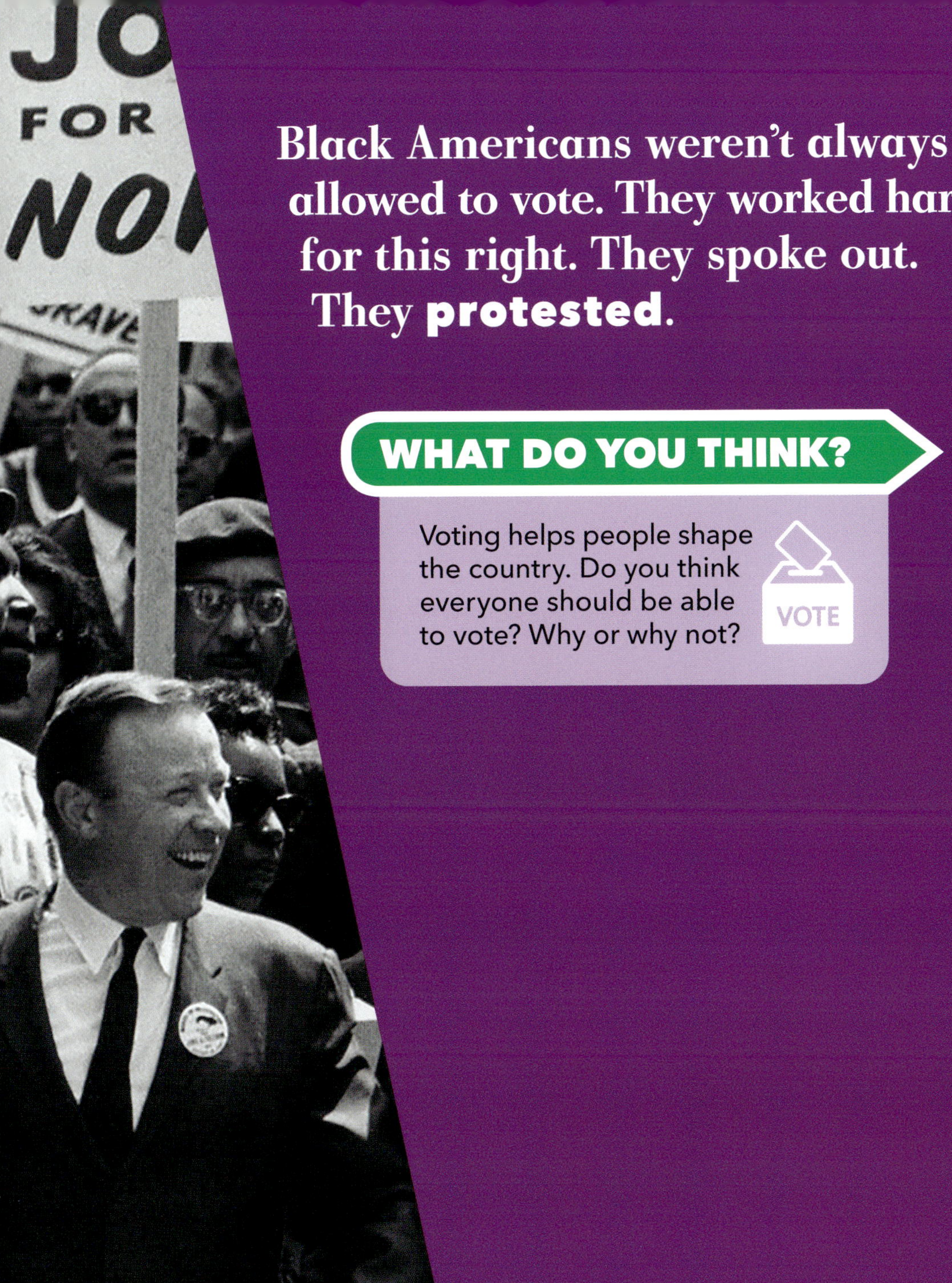

Black Americans weren't always allowed to vote. They worked hard for this right. They spoke out. They **protested**.

WHAT DO YOU THINK?

Voting helps people shape the country. Do you think everyone should be able to vote? Why or why not?

VOTE

CHAPTER 2

THE LONG ROAD TO VOTE

For hundreds of years, many Black people in North America were **enslaved**. They were forced to work for white people. They were treated very badly. Black people could not vote for change.

Americans fought each other in the Civil War (1861–1865). Some people wanted slavery. Others did not. In the end, all Black people were freed. In 1870, the Fifteenth **Amendment** was added to the **U.S. Constitution**. It said Black men could vote.

Black men turned in their ballots. Southern states did not like this. They passed laws. The laws made it hard for Black people to vote. Some Black people had to pay to vote. Others had to pass hard tests. White people scared people of color out of voting. This went on for many years.

DID YOU KNOW?

Women got the right to vote in 1920. But state laws made it hard for Black women to vote.

VOTING RIGHTS FOR ALL!

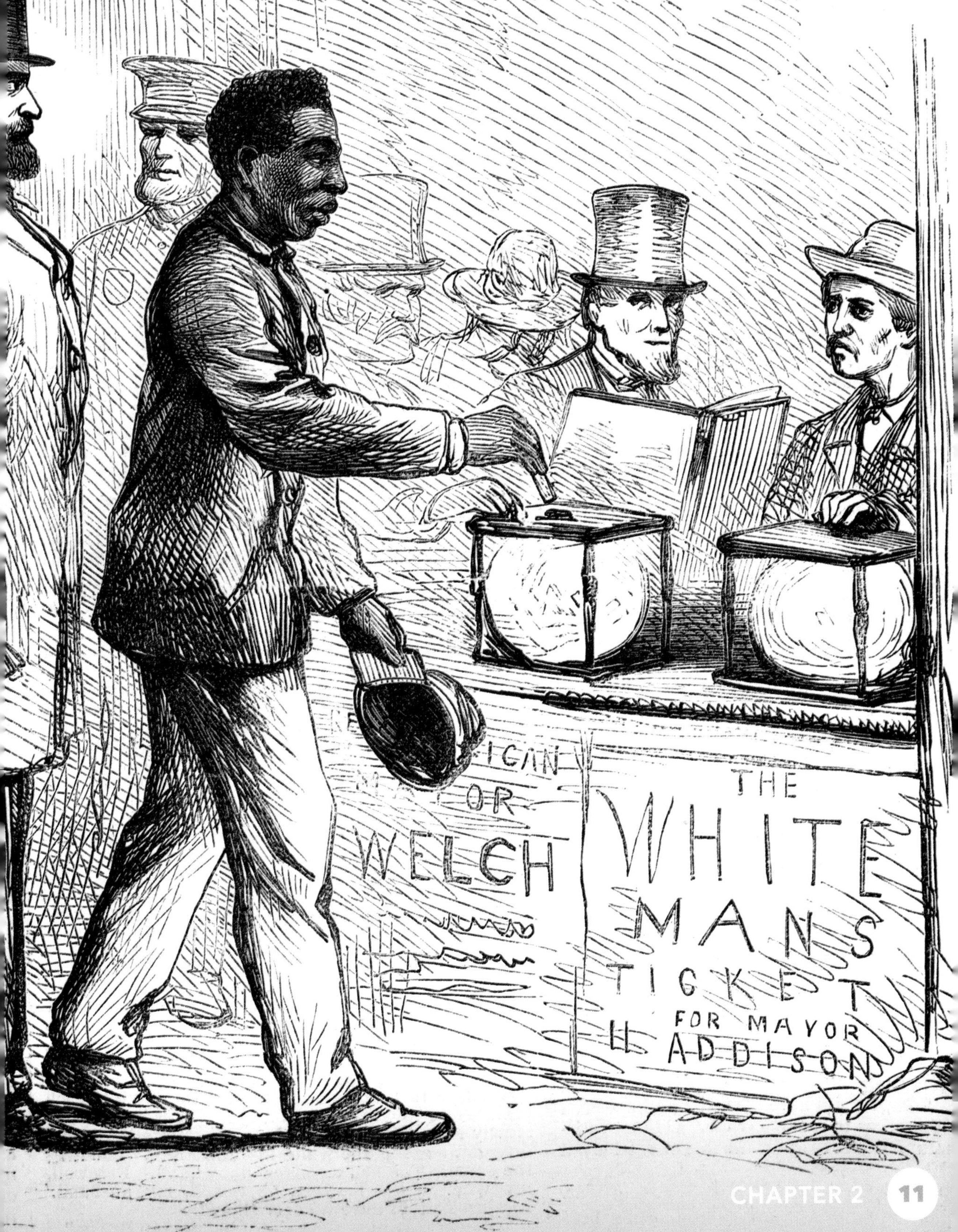
WELCH
THE
WHITE
MANS
TICKET
FOR MAYOR
ADDISON

Fannie Lou Hamer

Many Black people fought for voting rights. Fannie Lou Hamer was one. In 1963, she helped sign Black people up to vote. She was arrested and beaten. Two years later, Hamer gave a powerful speech. It was on TV. She spoke about what happened to her. People were shocked. Hamer kept working for change.

Dr. Martin Luther King, Jr. also worked for Black people's **civil rights**. How? He led peaceful protests. He wanted to end laws that kept Black people from voting. He gave many important speeches.

In 1965, **Congress** passed the Voting Rights Act. President Lyndon B. Johnson signed it. It became law. It said everyone could vote. People celebrated! More Black people were able to vote. They picked leaders who **represented** them.

33

CHAPTER 3

VOTING TODAY

In 2013, the U.S. **Supreme Court** made a decision. It took away some parts of the Voting Rights Act.

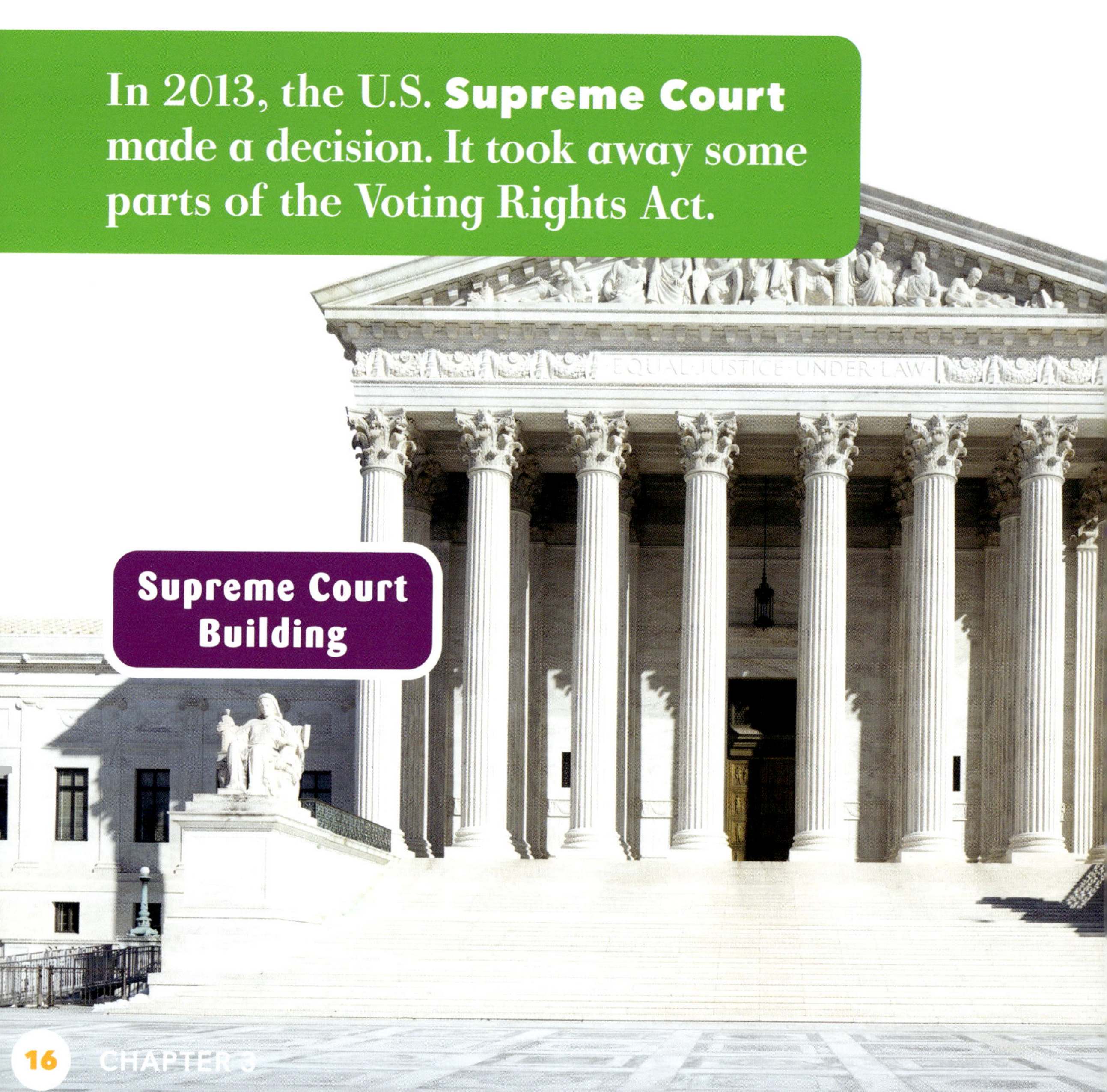

Supreme Court Building

States can now make voting laws. These laws often make it hard for Black people to vote. For example, some Black people do not have a **photo ID**. Some states require a photo ID to vote. Black people without one cannot vote in these states.

Many people vote at **polling places**. But some states closed them in Black neighborhoods. People there must travel to vote. They wait in longer lines. This makes voting hard.

WHAT DO YOU THINK?

Besides voting, what can you do to make your voice heard?

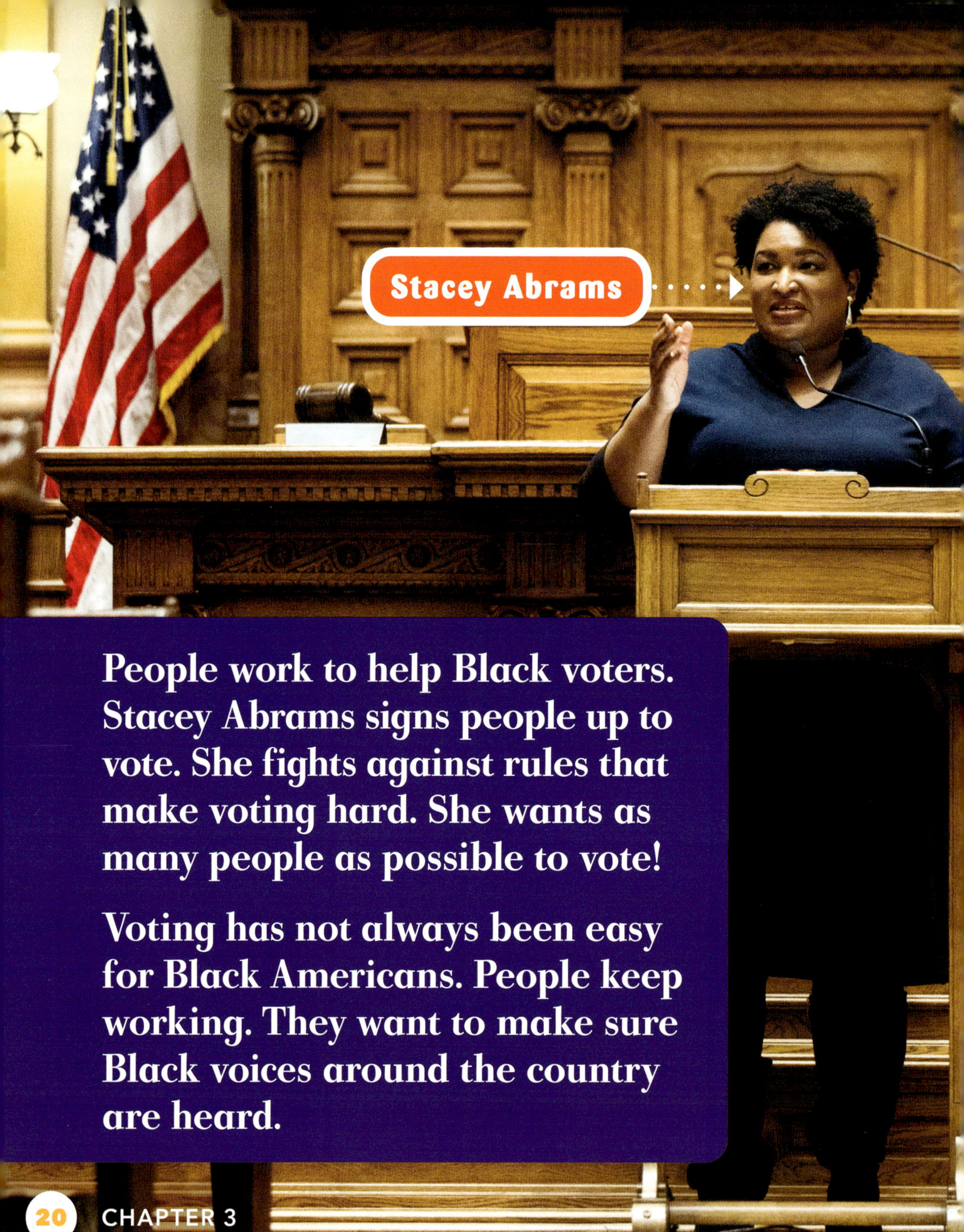

People work to help Black voters. Stacey Abrams signs people up to vote. She fights against rules that make voting hard. She wants as many people as possible to vote!

Voting has not always been easy for Black Americans. People keep working. They want to make sure Black voices around the country are heard.

TAKE A LOOK!

The graph below shows the percentage of U.S. Black citizens who voted for presidents between 1964 and 2020. Why do you think some years have more voters than others?

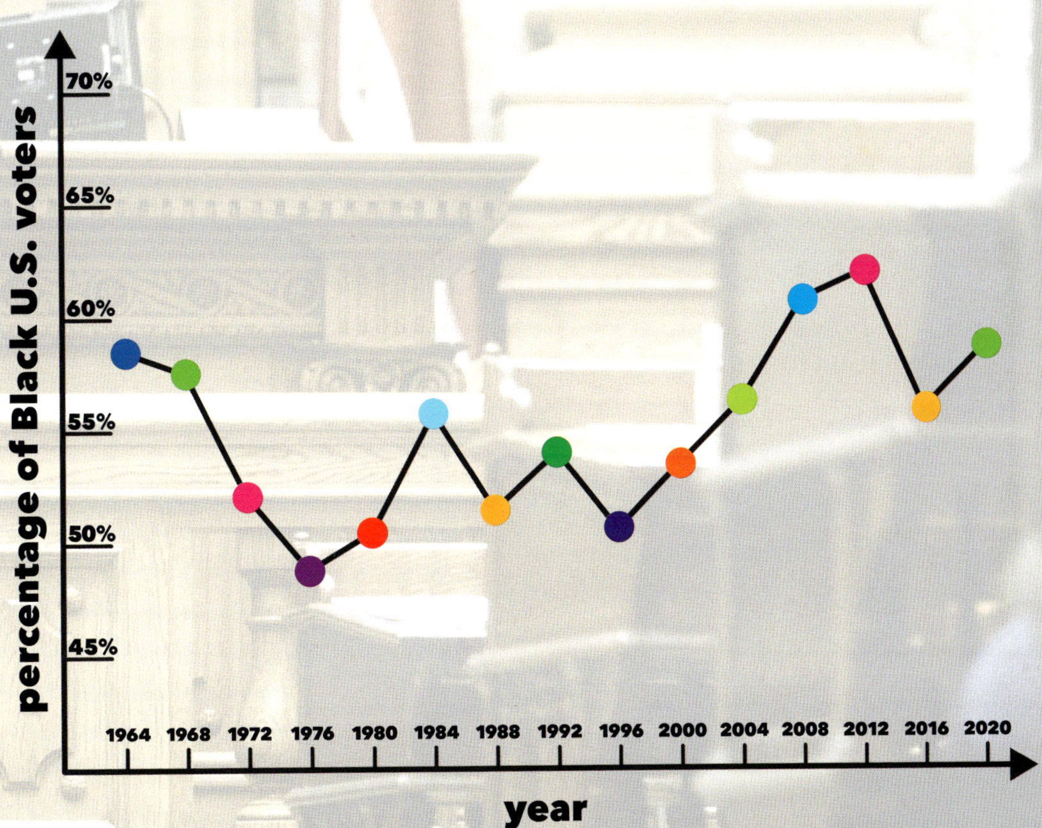

QUICK FACTS & TOOLS

TIMELINE

Black Americans have faced many struggles and successes when voting in the United States. Take a look.

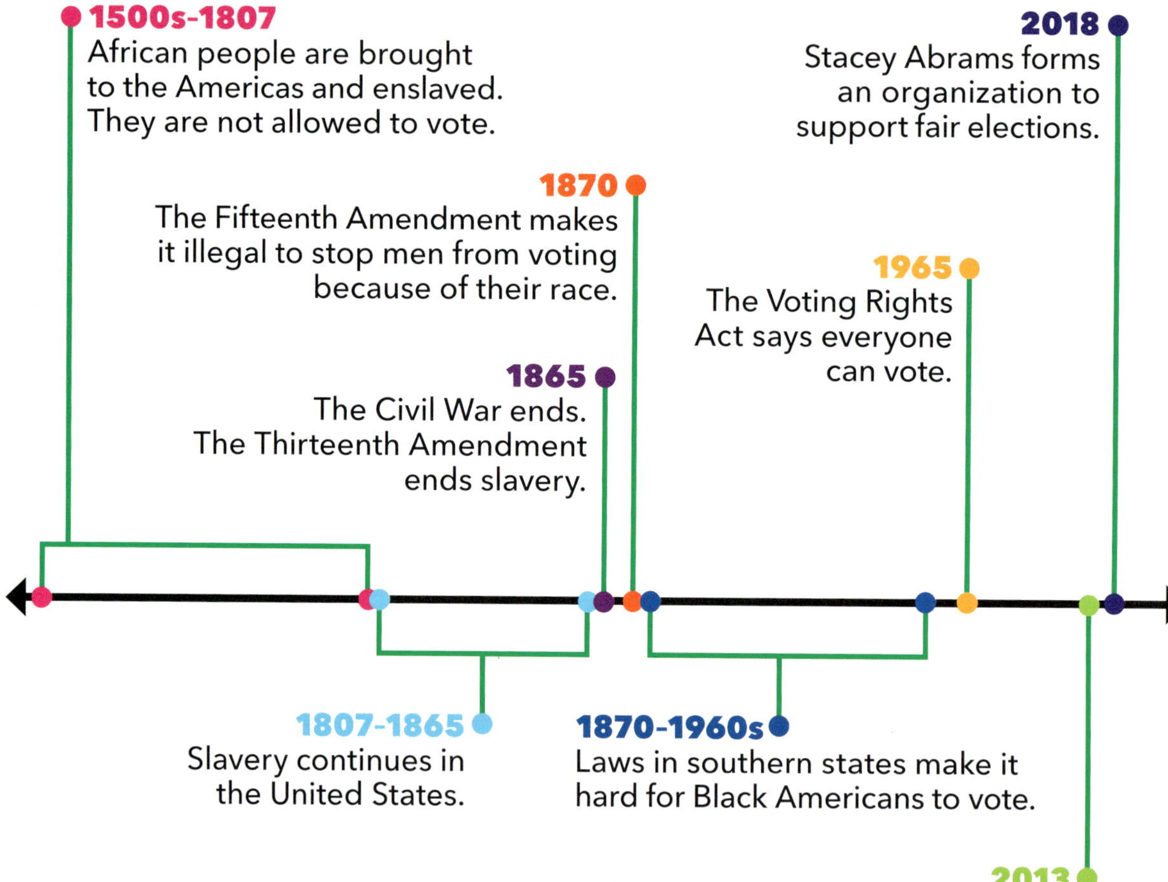

GLOSSARY

amendment: A change made to a law or legal document.

ballots: Pieces of paper that people use to mark which political candidates they want to hold office.

candidate: Someone who runs for office in an election.

citizens: People who belong to a country and have full rights.

civil rights: The individual rights that all members of a democratic society have to freedom and equal treatment under the law.

Congress: The branch of the U.S. government that makes laws.

democracy: A type of government in which people choose their leaders by voting in elections.

elections: The acts or processes of deciding something by voting.

enslaved: Forced to work without freedom or rights.

photo ID: A type of identification that includes a photograph.

polling places: Buildings or locations at which people vote.

protested: Demonstrated or made statements against something.

represented: Spoke or acted for someone else.

Supreme Court: The branch of the U.S. government that upholds the U.S. Constitution and laws.

U.S. Constitution: A written document containing the principles on how the United States should be governed.

INDEX

TO LEARN MORE

Finding more information is as easy as 1, 2, 3.

1. Go to www.factsurfer.com
2. Enter "BlackAmericans'righttovote" into the search box.
3. Choose your book to see a list of websites.